THE ADVENTURES OF BUTTERS AND TWEAK

STORY BY DONNA SHELTON AND LAURA KOLINSKY

ILLUSTRATED BY CATT BUKO

Copyright © 2023
All Rights Reserved

About the Authors

Authors Donna Shelton and Laura Kolinsky are a mother daughter duo, with this being their first book. Donna was always writing poems for her daughters for fun, and always dreamed of having her own series for kids. Laura's two cats, Butters and Tweak, were the perfect subject matter. Combined with Laura's passion for rescue animals, a book series was born. They look forward to sharing the many adventures of Butters and Tweak and introducing their many friends to children worldwide.

Butters and Tweak are two very special cats adopted from the longest running cage free, no-kill, cat shelter in the United States, The Ellen M. Gifford Cat Shelter in Boston, Massachusetts.

We hope you enjoy their adventures and are inspired to adopt those often-overlooked pets.

Butters and Tweak were friends right from the start.
They met in a cat shelter where they were seldom apart.

For none of the shelter kitties liked one or the other.
So, they clung to each other like sister and brother.

Butters was a big cat; they called him "The Lump". The other cats stayed away from him because he was rather plump.

And Tweak was so pretty with a coat that was shiny. But no one liked her either because of the problem with her hiney.

You see, when she was nervous, there were strange rumblings in her belly,

That made her hiney emit a scary noise, and boy was it SMELLY!

"No one will want to adopt us," of this, they were sure.
Their feelings of hopelessness they felt to the core.

But one day, two humans came and saw the pair.
Tweak and Butters hoped they would be the answer to their prayer.

Both were adopted, much to their glee.

Together with the humans, they would be one happy family.

But Tweak's delight soon turned to dismay,
As it became apparent that her "problem" wasn't going away.

Tweak worried that the humans would, indeed, mind,
Even though they had proved that they were truly kind.

Now it so happened on one frightful day,
An intruder came into their home with every intention to stay.

Razzi, the neighborhood rat, showed up at their door,
And walked right in and strode across the floor.

Tweak reacted with a mighty hiss,
And said to Razzi, "We'll have none of this."

But she got so nervous, there were rumblings in her belly,
And out of her hiney came that scary noise again, and boy, was it SMELLY!

With a look of disgust, Razzi ran from the house and into the street,

And kept going as fast as he could on his little rat feet.

The humans hugged Tweak and said that she was a dear.

And that she had a home with them forever; she had nothing to fear!

The end...

...of this adventure of Butters and Tweak.

www.ingramcontent.com/pod-product-compliance
Lightning Source LLC
Chambersburg PA
CBHW042107090526
44590CB00004B/129